NORTH CAROLINA
STATE BOARD OF COMMUNITY COLLEGES
LIBRARIES
ASHEVILLE-BUNCOMBE TECHNICAL COMMUNITY COLLEGE

DISCARDED

AUG 4 2025

D1000447

First Lady of the Senate

A Life of

MARGARET CHASE SMITH

A WINDSWEPT BOOK
Windswept House Publishers
Mt. Desert, Maine

Copyright 1990 by Alberta Gould
Library of Congress Catalog # 89-51315
ISBN 0-932433-64-2

Printed for the publisher by
Downeast Graphics & Printing, Inc.
Ellsworth, Maine

For

Michelle, Lisa, David, and Peter

"My creed is that public service must be more than doing a job efficiently and honestly. It must be a complete dedication to the people and to the nation with full recognition that every human being is entitled to courtesy and consideration, that constructive criticism is not only to be expected but sought, that smears are not only to be expected, but fought, that honor is to be earned but not bought."

MARGARET CHASE SMITH
November 11, 1953

INTRODUCTION

Due to my life-long fascination with history and deep admiration for Senator Margaret Chase Smith, I have written this book with a two-fold purpose.

First, to make young people aware of the Senator's life and accomplishments. Not merely the events of her ninety odd years, but beyond that, the aspects of her character and personality that we need to see in other public officials of today.

Secondly, it is my hope that teachers will make use of this book in their classroom studies of United States history. Since it spans close to one-half of the time the United States has been a nation, a great deal of our history can be seen through the Senator's eyes.

I have recently observed an increased interest in some schools to teach our young people the lessons of history through the eyes of those who made that history. If we fail to do this, we shall doom them to repeat our mistakes.

The Author

FOREWORD BY SENATOR GEORGE MITCHELL

Maine people have long had the reputation of being independent. Few Mainers have deserved that reputation more than one of our most famous citizens, former Senator Margaret Chase Smith.

The events of her life are all described in this biography. But the trait I most admire and respect about Senator Margaret Chase Smith is her independence of judgment. That was demonstrated by the courage she showed thirty-nine years ago, in 1950, in speaking her mind.

We most often see courage reflected in action. Early colonists fighting to protect their homesteads, Revolutionary War soldiers fighting against the world's greatest military power two hundred years ago, the Union Army volunteers who won the Civil War that kept our nation unified — all these episodes in our history contain examples of extraordinary personal bravery and sacrifice that are still admired today.

We do not often think about courage in connection with making a speech.

But at the time when Senator Margaret Chase Smith made what is called her "Declaration of Conscience", it did, indeed, take enormous courage to stand up and simply tell the truth.

Our nation is based on the principle that each American has certain fundamental rights, including the right to have unpopular ideas or express unpopular views. That is our ideal. But, in practice, we do not always live up to the ideal.

It was during such a time that Senator Margaret Chase Smith had the courage to remind our country of its ideals.

In 1950, our nation was only five years out of the most destructive war of all time, World War II. Hundreds of thousands of Americans died in that war, millions were wounded, and millions of civilians all over the world lost lives, homes, property and their very countries because of it.

But our victory in 1945 did not bring peace. Instead, it brought the beginning of what is called the Cold War — a period in which America and the nations of Western Europe were faced with a real and serious Soviet threat.

At that time, anger and fear combined to make most Americans think that communism was a threat to our way of life which had to be fought by any means possible. People whose loyalties were suspect or challenged lost their jobs. Some were hounded out of their communities. Some lives were wrecked, some reputations lost.

There *were* real dangers from communism. But there were also unfounded rumors and irresponsible charges. The nation was in danger of forgetting the fundamental principle of American justice: innocent until proven guilty.

Indeed, in that time, most Americans, whatever they thought privately, refused in public even to defend the principle of fairness, for fear of being accused of sympathizing with communism.

But one of the most important strengths of America is our freedom to disagree openly with each other. One of the traits that makes patriots out of Americans is our knowledge that no matter what our opinions, our system of laws and justice respects our right to hold those opinions.

Senator Smith was the first to remind Americans of that fact. She was the first to stand up against the witch-hunting atmosphere of the times and speak out strongly for the right of all Americans to be treated fairly. She reminded her colleagues in the Senate and all Americans that our nation is strongest when it holds most firmly to its ideals.

It takes courage of a special kind to stand up when the majority of people are afraid. It is not easy to stand up for the rights of people who are unpopular.

The courage to speak your own mind when doing so risks your reputation and even your job is courage of a quiet kind. It is different from the bravery displayed in combat. But it can be just as difficult. It is courage of an unusual type, and in Senator Margaret Chase Smith, Maine had an elected official with that kind of courage.

Prologue

It is nine in the morning on a sunny day in June. At the Margaret Chase Smith Library Center overlooking the placid Kennebec River in Skowhegan, Maine, there is a quiet hum of activity. The receptionist has already taken phone calls and begun scheduling appointments for the library staff.

Senator Smith has been up for hours. An early riser, 5:45 a.m. at the latest, she is tastefully dressed in a blue suit, a fresh red rose on her lapel. She's looking forward to one of her favorite activities. A group of fourth-grade students and their teacher will be visiting the center.

Even at age ninety, she still enjoys the curious, talkative, elementary age children. She can anticipate their questions and predict what will capture their attention in the museum. They will want to know about the models, one a spacecraft, the other a supersonic jet. There are over two hundred miniature elephants in the glass cases. One question asked over and over by the various students, "Is the elephant your favorite animal?"

This always brings a smile to her face as she reflects on the symbol of the Republican Party, which first appeared in an 1874 cartoon by Thomas Nast in *Harper's Weekly*.

The elephant represented the Republican vote. Nast used elephants many times as a Republican symbol and it soon came to stand for the Republican Party.

Moving deliberately along the wide hall of the museum, she glances from left to right at the displays. Mementos of her years in Washington, pictures of hometown landmarks, photos of famous people, books, and elephants . . . elephants . . . elephants!

One of the most impressive and colorful displays is Senator Smith's collection of honorary degree hoods. Ninety-two colleges and universities have granted her doctorates. This self-taught woman who could not afford to go to college now holds many honorary degrees such as Doctor of Law, Doctor of Philosophy, and of Education.

Memory flickers like a high-speed movie. And she has a lot to remember! However, she doesn't live in the past. She could have retired to her Skowhegan home, taken up needlework, and settled into a comfortable rocker, but that is not her style. Active, articulate, and witty, she continues to share her life with the public, from school children to admiring politicians.

Senator Smith steps into the conference room where the children are waiting. Introductions are made and within minutes, everyone feels like old friends.

I

The Margaret Chase Smith Library Center is only a short distance from Margaret's birthplace. Although the distance is short, a great deal of time and history has passed between Margaret's birth on December 14, 1897 and her ninetieth birthday celebration in 1987!

No one dreamed on the day Margaret was born that ninety years later, some of the nation's most powerful people would be paying honor to the country girl from central Maine.

What was it about her family life that instilled honesty, plain speech, and independence in her?

Who were the people who influenced her education and involvement in world affairs?

What was it about life in a small farming community that prepared Margaret for greatness?

Margaret has many happy memories of her homelife. She was born the eldest of six children. Two brothers died in childhood, leaving Margaret, Wilbur, Evelyn, and Laura.

Some of Margaret's favorite childhood escapades were

done in the company of her best friend, Pauline Bragg. The girls would visit back and forth at each other's homes, or perhaps take a walk downtown to look in the windows of the stores that lined Water Street.

Papa Chase was a barber, with his shop next to their home on North Avenue. The shop was an intriguing place with its huge mirror that nearly covered an entire wall. Each customer who paid Papa Chase for his daily shave kept a shaving mug at the shop with his name printed on it in gold letters.

Margaret had great love and respect for her parents. They were of Irish, English, Scotch, and French-Canadian background. Margaret says of her mother, "She was strong-minded and exerted great influence over us children. She taught us to appreciate everything we had, to work hard, and obey her and Papa."

The Chase home did not boast any luxuries, as they were not rich. But there was plenty of food on the table and the children had the clothes they needed, even if they were not always an exact fit or the latest style.

Margaret remembers pitching in to help with chores at home. The girls were expected to sweep, dust, and iron clothes even when there were more enjoyable things to do. They did not receive an allowance, sometimes they would be given a few pennies for a special treat, or be paid for doing an extra chore.

The money Margaret earned doing chores did not last long. She and Pauline would often run to the corner store to buy a box of chocolate, coconut, marshmallow cremes. By the time they got home, the box would be empty!

Luckily, it did not cost anything to stroll to the red brick public library on Elm Street. Margaret and Pauline regularly borrowed their favorite books.

One memorable tradition of Margaret's childhood was hanging May baskets. On the first day of May, Margaret and her brother, Wilbur, would get up early. They had made elaborate preparations the night before. Little baskets had been constructed with colored paper, flowers or ribbons, and filled with gumdrops. Wilbur and Margaret would slip quietly down the street to their friend's homes where they would hang the baskets on the door knob. After yelling, "May basket!" they would run and hide. As soon as their friends found the May basket, they would search for Margaret and Wilbur. When everyone had been found, the treats in the basket were passed around.

Margaret recalls a time when most of the young girls in Skowhegan wore their hair in long curls held in place with ribbons. However, the "Dutch-cut" became the rage. Not to be left out, Margaret persuaded her father to give her the fashionable new haircut. Whether or not Margaret's mother knew ahead of time about this plan, all she said when Margaret returned home was, "Oooh, Margaret!"

Life moved at a slow, leisurely pace in the late 1800's. Movies and television were not yet invented. In Skowhegan, automobiles were a rare sight. The jet plane was a dream of the future.

Summer was the children's favorite time of year. School was out and they did not have to go to bed as early. With shouting and laughter echoing through the neighborhood, they would gather in front of the nearby Universalist Church for games of hide-and-seek or giant step.

Winter or summer, birthdays were made special by Papa and Mama Chase. There was a big party . . . not an ordinary one! Sometimes there would be as many as eighty children. Margaret's parents would invite all the neighborhood children who did not ordinarily go to birthday parties. There would be homemade ice cream in the crank freezer. Everyone would take a turn at the crank until it would turn no longer. The child who cranked last would be allowed to lick the paddle.

Many weekends during the summer, the Chase family would make the trip by horse and buckboard to their rented cabin on North Pond in Smithfield for lazy hours of swimming and fishing. Leaving Skowhegan after closing the barber shop on Saturday night, they would arrive at their cabin by ten p.m. "We all went to bed. But at four a.m. my father would ask who was up," Margaret recalls. The rest of the family slept on, but Margaret would struggle out of bed and go trolling for perch with Papa. He would clean them on the rocks and they would be ready for the frypan just about the time the others got up.

In spite of the lack of outside entertainments, the children were seldom bored. They found something fun to do in simple activities, like raking leaves in the fall and jumping into huge mounds.

Bundled up in layers of long-johns, mufflers, and mittens, like Arctic explorers, they would spend evenings and weekends during the winter, sledding, ice skating or building snowmen.

Christmas brought special treats. Every year the Chases went into the nearby woods to cut their tree. After much debate over size and shape, they would find the "perfect" tree, cut it down, and carry it home to be set up in the parlor.

Decorating the tree was a highlight for Margaret. The family would gather around the kitchen table to string popcorn and red cranberries into garlands. Mama Chase would fill little, green cheesecloth bags with an orange and hang them on the branches. Candy canes and a homemade star on top would complete the decorations.

On Christmas morning there would be a pile of packages under the tree, but there were no fancy or expensive gifts. With four children, the boxes usually contained stockings, night clothes, or a brush and comb.

Margaret's parents wanted their children to have a good time, but have it at home! They did not mind having half of the young people in Skowhegan under foot in the house or barn playing games, dancing, or putting on plays.

Skowhegan's youngsters looked forward to the State Fair every August. Margaret and her friends would make the long hike to the fairgrounds. As they walked the midway with a few coins jingling in their pockets, Margaret had to make some agonizing choices. Should she ride the ferris wheel and buy cotton candy, or the carousel and eat roasted peanuts? She couldn't afford everything. She promised herself that someday she would earn her own money!

Soon after this, Margaret convinced the manager of Green Brothers Five and Ten Cent Store to consider her as a sales clerk. There was only one flaw in this grand idea. Twelve year old Margaret was too short to reach the shelves! Undaunted, Margaret would secretly measure herself against the stacks of boxes on the shelves every time she went into Green Brothers.

A whole year passed before she grew tall enough to reach the topmost shelves, standing on tiptoe. When the day finally came, and she was hired at ten cents an hour, it was an excited Margaret who ran home to break the news to her family. Another surprise was in store as her mother no longer required her to do household chores now that she was a "working girl."

To the delight of both girls, Pauline Bragg soon joined Margaret at Green Brothers.

Looking back, Margaret says, "I was always a very independent child and preferred to work. I was also a curious one. I wanted experiences."

II

Because she lived on the North side of Skowhegan, Margaret attended the Lincoln and Garfield elementary schools. These two buildings were around the corner from her home. Margaret's sharp memory came in handy at spelling bees and learning poetry, but she did not enjoy English grammar.

One of her treasures, yellowed with age, is a piece of paper with the signatures of all her second grade classmates.

After passing through the Lincoln and Garfield schools, Margaret and her neighborhood friends had a longer walk to the large, square, red brick high school. It was located on an island in the Kennebec River, connected to the mainland by two bridges. It was this very site that gave Skowhegan its name. Indian legend claims the Norridgewock tribe watched for fish at the double waterfalls, one each end of the island. Skowhegan means, "the place to watch for fish."

In 1977 Skowhegan renamed the North Channel and the South Channel bridges in her honor. Never had she imagined any such distinction when she and her chums passed over the bridges on their way to high school!

Margaret, Pauline, and a few other girls in their class

studied the commercial course in high school. The typing, shorthand, and bookkeeping would prepare them to go directly to work after graduation.

Margaret was already employed, having spent Friday evenings and all day Saturday at Green Brothers for the past two years.

True to her claim of being curious, Margaret would sometimes visit a friend who had worked as a switchboard operator for the Maine Telephone and Telegraph Company. She thought it was fun learning to push the proper plug into the correct hole to connect callers. Once in awhile her friend would be out sick and Margaret was knowledgeable enough to fill in. Nevertheless, it was a surprise when she was asked to train as a substitute night switchboard operator! Even though the pay was the same as at Green Brothers, this was a major step up. The switchboard operator was highly respected and knew everyone in town.

One of the most frequent callers on Margaret's evening duty was First Selectman Clyde Smith. At age twenty-one, he had become the youngest man to be elected sheriff of Somerset County. Now, in his thirties, he was the most important man in town. Clyde Smith had a habit of calling the telephone operator to find out the correct time. Margaret was impressed with his voice and manner and always tried to answer him with dignity and accuracy.

In the spring of her senior year, Margaret received a call from Clyde Smith. This time he did not ask her the correct time, but instead offered her the job of recording tax payments in the town books. The salary was double what she was earning as a telephone operator and she would still receive credit for her courses, as seniors were allowed to get on-the-job training. She accepted the position.

Another special privilege for the seniors was a trip to Washington, D.C., the nation's capitol. Margaret was determined to go, but lacked the sixty dollars. As she tells it, "My grandfather Murray asked me to meet him in front of the Skowhegan Savings Bank one day to help him with an errand. We went into the bank and he asked Mr. Merrill, a bank officer, for sixty dollars and a note. He then asked Mr. Merrill to make it at six percent interest. I was to pay back the sixty dollars along with the six percent interest, and I did. At first I was disappointed that he did not give the money to me. But this taught me the full value of money and that was a great lesson! I'm sure I got more out of the trip because I had to pay for it myself."

When the train pulled out of the Skowhegan station bound for Washington, D.C., Margaret was one of those aboard. Anticipation was high since most of the students had never traveled further than Waterville, twenty miles away.

In Washington, a Congressman named John Peters took the seniors to visit the national landmarks. Margaret and her classmates were awed by the Washington Monument and the White House. The various exhibits at the Smithsonian Institution fascinated the students. They were also welcomed into the home of a well-known public figure. There Margaret had a special treat. For the first time, she ate vanilla, strawberry, and chocolate ice cream together from the same package. It was called harlequin.

She recalls, "I did not know what well-known political people were like, but there I spent time with them and shook their hands. I found them to be human, just like my friends and neighbors back home. It left a lasting impression."

After graduation, some of Margaret's classmates were going to college. But with three younger children in the family, George and Carrie Chase couldn't afford to send Margaret. Her dream of becoming a gym teacher would have to wait until she earned enough money to pay her own way.

Margaret hoped for a full-time telephone operator's job following graduation, but none were open. So she accepted a teaching position in a one-room building in a rural area known as the Pitt School. The pay was $8.50 per week. These days such a job would require four years of college training, at least, but in 1916 the small rural schools of Maine required determination and a high school diploma.

There were nine students in eight grades and it was a challenge that required all of Margaret's determination. She said, "I enjoyed it, but I didn't have enough time with the students. I figured it out one day, and I only had two minutes a day per student per subject! I couldn't do very much. I also learned I had not studied to teach and I didn't know how. I was smart enough to realize that!"

Margaret stayed with a farm family during the week, walking to and from the school through the snowdrifts every day. She paid five dollars for room and board at the farm. On Friday nights, she would be back in Skowhegan to coach the girls basketball team. Being an independent young woman, Margaret insisted on paying her mother $1.50 for board at home for the weekend, leaving $2.00 for herself.

With spring, came the welcome news that an operator's job had opened up. Luckily, a substitute teacher was found for the rest of the term and Margaret moved back home to her mother's homemade biscuits and her familiar stool at the switchboard. Margaret was also working with her best friend Pauline again!

As the Chase children grew older, they traded in their weekly trips to Smithfield's North Pond for the enjoyable experience of taking the trolly car from town to nearby Wesserunsett Lake. Papa Chase built a small cottage. The family went fishing, picnicking, or for a ride on the steamboat around the lake. A summer theatre and band concerts added to the fun. Margaret's crowd of friends spent many delightful summer evenings strolling the grounds or just chatting on the front porch of the hotel.

A short time after going back to the telephone office, she was faced with another decision. She could either move up to the position of chief operator, or work in the business office. The office job was her choice.

As time passed, Margaret discovered her interest in becoming a gym teacher was evaporating just like the money she was trying to save. Besides, she enjoyed being a businesswoman!

Two years later, she was offered a job as circulation manager for the town's weekly newspaper, the *Independ-*

ent Reporter. As a "newswoman", Margaret tried her hand at many jobs. When she discovered she was unfamiliar with writing ads, she bought an edition of the *New York Times* to see how it was done! She was also credited with coining the paper's slogan: "There are eleven Bostons, many Londons, but only one Skowhegan."

When Margaret was twenty-five, she traveled with a group of secretaries and businesswomen to Portland, Maine. There she listened to a speech by the national president of the Business and Professional Women's Club. The young women of Skowhegan returned home from that meeting very excited and determined to start a club of their own. They rented rooms on the second floor of a downtown office building and began meeting twice a month. To help cover their expenses, they rented their piano to a local piano teacher for her lessons.

In its second year, Margaret was elected president. One of her programs was to ask the ladies to stand up in front of the group, give their name, describe their jobs, and other details of their lives. Margaret felt this exercise would help them to learn to speak in public.

In 1926, she was elected to serve as the president of the Business and Professional Woman's Club of Maine. She was the youngest, and turned out to be one of the most popular.

The many friends she made during those days became a major support later when she ran for public office. But all that was far in the future.

Margaret enjoyed her work at the newspaper, especially

a new feature she had created, a job service. Her contacts with the local businessmen as the circulation manager had given her the idea of starting a column that matched employers with prospective employees.

However, when a job as office manager at the Cummings Woolen Mill became available, she applied. The job paid fifty dollars a week, nearly double what she was earning at the newspaper. She was hired, and those years of managing a staff gave Margaret valuable experience for the years ahead.

She tells young people today, "All those working experiences I had with people counted greatly many years later when I was in Congress. I had to be organized, and I had to get along with people."

Margaret's years at the paper had renewed an old acquaintance. Clyde Smith was now a state senator. Margaret was an attractive, successful businesswoman. Their friendship grew into a special relationship.

III

"I don't know that Clyde ever courted me, it was a gradual thing," Margaret said.

Clyde Smith, divorced and a professional politician, was fifty-four. He was born in Harmony, Maine and had served in numerous appointed and elected public offices. He had gained a reputation for being hard-working, energetic, and daring.

Margaret was thirty-three, pretty, and respected by her employers and many friends. The age difference didn't matter, they were a perfect match.

Margaret smiles as she recalls her parents reaction to her dating an older man. "They weren't pleased, but they saw I was determined, so they went along."

As Clyde and Margaret dated, they were too mature and too busy to go dancing and to movies like most other couples. Instead, Margaret would accompany Clyde on the campaign trail. She thought it was exciting to sit on the front row and listen to his speeches. Meeting new people was also stimulating and fun. She had never been particularly interested in politics, but with Clyde explaining it to her, she found it to be a very exciting subject!

Margaret and Clyde set their wedding day for May 4, 1930. The short ceremony was performed in the parlor of the Chase home. Margaret carried a bouquet of roses and was attended by her two sisters, Evelyn and Laura.

After the service, the reception was held across town at the Smith family home, a thirty room mansion. The huge living room, dining room and reception hall were filled to capacity with family and friends. Standing in the receiving line, accepting congratulations from their guests, reminded Margaret of campaigning!

Margaret was sure she would enjoy married life. With Clyde, it would not be dull. One thing already pleased her. That was the sound of her new name . . . Margaret Chase Smith.

At the time of their marriage, Clyde was Chairman of the State Highway Commission. In 1932 he was elected to the Governor's Council.

Margaret gave up her business career to become a full-time politician's wife. She joined the Republican State Committee, the organization that was responsible for helping candidates get elected. Clyde and Margaret spent many hours driving in their big, black Maxwell to every corner of Maine. They renewed old acquaintances and made many new friends.

Margaret had no idea when she gave up her career three months after her marriage, that her life would never be the same again. She was very busy keeping house in her large new home. Friends, associates, public officials were dropping by their home frequently, and Margaret was a gracious hostess.

Realization came slowly as to what a public official's life would be like. Yes, it was often exciting and fun. But it was also hard work and there were many sacrifices.

There were the family times that a public servant misses because he has responsibilities elsewhere. There are the events and celebrations of everyday life that pass by in the hustle and bustle of the politician's busy days. When people give themselves to serve the public in an elected or appointed office, their time becomes public property and their energy is directed to meeting the needs they have committed themselves to support.

Gradually, Margaret began to understand this.

Often Clyde was required to travel to Augusta, the State Capitol, on business. Margaret would go along and sit in the hall of the Capitol building, knitting or reading while Clyde was busy in a meeting.

Clyde considered running for Governor of Maine in 1936, but the Republican Party leaders persuaded him to run for Congress instead. More trips, more speeches, more shaking hands, and once again Clyde won the election! He was now Congressman Clyde Smith from Maine's Second District and would need to spend most of the year in Washington, D.C.

IV

With mixed feelings, Clyde and Margaret Smith left Skowhegan for Washington, D.C. As the hills and forests receded into the distance, an exciting adventure lay ahead.

Clyde and Margaret were caught up in a whirlwind of activity upon their arrival in the Capitol. Settling into their new home, putting Clyde's office in order, and meeting new people kept Margaret busy. In addition, Clyde decided Margaret should be his "official" secretary, since they had worked so well together for the past six years. The job was not easy. The telephone and mail were demanding, researching information for Clyde's votes, and some fact-finding trips kept Margaret at work twelve to fifteen hours a day.

Of all these activities, one of the Smiths' favorites was hosting the hundreds of seniors who visited Washington every spring from high schools in Maine. They received the "red carpet" treatment from Clyde and Margaret, who having no children of their own, thoroughly enjoyed the young people.

Three years after being elected to Congress, Clyde suffered a heart attack. As he rested at their Washington home, Margaret was at his bedside every day. She would take dictation as Clyde answered his mail, then later at night, she would type the letters. Clyde continued his interest in politics and his work was uppermost in his thoughts.

Since he was up for re-election in the June Primary, Clyde began to worry about whether or not he would be well enough to campaign for re-election. It was Clyde's doctor who suggested that Margaret should file the necessary papers for the June Primary in Clyde's place. Dr. Dickins convinced her by explaining that it would keep Clyde from worrying about the election. The plan was, that once Clyde recovered, Margaret would withdraw, and Clyde would resume his place on the ballot.

After contacting a number of other prominent Congressmen and friends for their opinions, Margaret hesitantly agreed that this would be best for Clyde.

On April 7, Clyde prepared a news release notifying the press that Margaret would file for the June Primary in place of her ill husband. Even as the statement was being transmitted, Clyde suffered a second heart attack. This time Dr. Dickins was unable to save his patient. Within hours, Margaret had lost her husband and closest friend.

Margaret hardly had time to grieve, since there was so much to be done. Clyde Smith had been a popular man in his home state and well liked in Congress. Margaret took Clyde's body back to Maine for the large funeral. She bravely accepted the sympathetic gestures of their many relatives and friends.

3028 Newark Street,
Washington, D.C. April 7, 1940.

On Wednesday, April the third, 1940, about midnight, I was suddenly taken ill with heart disease, called by the doctor, coronary thrombosis. My physician, Doctor Paul F. Dickens, informs me that I am a seriously ill man, that it is his opinion that even though I survive, I may be physically unable to take an active part in Congressional affairs for an indefinite time in the future.

Therefore in loyalty to my friends, my district, to the state of Maine and to my party, I have requested that my wife, Margaret Chase Smith also enter the primary, filing three for which closes April 15th.

All that I can ask of my friends and supporters is that in the coming primary and general election, if unable to enter campaign, they support the candidate of my choice, my wife and my partner in public life, Margaret Chase Smith.

I know of no one else who has the full knowledge of my ideas and plans or is as well qualified as she is, to carry on these ideas and my unfinished work for my district.

This statement of my present physical condition and wishes is necessarily short and the reason therefor obvious.

Original draft of Congressman Clyde Smith's letter showing handwritten corrections.

Now she was faced with an unbelievable challenge! She had never planned to go into politics, but circumstances had thrust her into a position far beyond her expectations. She would much rather have been campaigning with Clyde, but she was alone. In his forty-eight tries for public office, he had never once lost an election. Being with him in some of those campaigns taught her that Clyde had put his all into campaigning, and so would she!

A May Primary was soon followed by a special election in June, in which Margaret was chosen to fill Clyde's unexpired term. After campaigning like a veteran, she went on to win the September election by an overwhelming vote. This time she left for Washington as a Congresswoman in her own right. January 6, 1941 was a proud day for Margaret as she was sworn into membership of the United States House of Representatives.

Margaret began a tradition after Clyde's death that she has continued all her life. She answered every letter and telegram of sympathy with a personal note.

"I started out answering my own mail. I don't like form letters and I never used a rubber stamp of my signature. No one else has ever been authorized to sign my name."

This practice has meant a lot of work, but it's the personal touch that had endeared Margaret to so many people.

Margaret with her parents, Carrie and George Chase.

Margaret at age six.

Margaret is (second from right) sitting in the second row with her fourth grade class.

The Chase home on North Avenue in Skowhegan.

Margaret (second from right) with her high school basketball team.

Margaret's high school diploma, 1916.

Margaret posed for this photo at her old job on the telephone switchboard.

Margaret's husband, Clyde Smith.

Representative Smith in her Washington office, 1947.

Margaret answering the daily mail at the Chase home in Skowhegan, 1947. (During House term.)

Margaret driving her own car during the 1948 Senate campaign.

Political cartoon used in the Chicago Tribune in the 1948 Senate campaign.

Margaret is sworn into office with a group of other freshmen Senators on January 4, 1949.

Senator Joseph R. McCarthy seated second from left presides at a hearing. Fourth and fifth from left are Senator Smith and her executive assistant, Bill Lewis.

President Harry S. Truman signs the bill, sponsored by Representative Smith, granting permanent status in the military to Army and Navy nurses, April 16, 1947.

Left to right: Margaret met with Prime Minister, Winston Churchill and Foreign Minister, Anthony Eden of England during the 1954 world tour.

V

Nineteen forty-one, the year Margaret entered the House of Representatives, was a year of world-wide crisis. On the continent of Europe, two growing military powers were dreaming of conquest.

Germany, ruled by the Nazi dictator, Adolph Hitler, and Italy under the domination of Fascist Benito Mussolini, had made a power-hungry alliance to rule the continent.

Even as Hitler was making speeches proclaiming his desire for peace, his "storm-troopers" were attacking the countries of Poland and Czechoslovakia. This was frightening news for the free countries of Europe. Across the English Channel in the British House of Commons, the growly voice of Winston Churchill was warning his countrymen that Hitler would eventually attempt an invasion of England.

Back home in Washington, Margaret and her fellow lawmakers had many tough decisions to make. One bill that caused a big uproar was President Roosevelt's Lend-Lease Act. This would permit the United States to loan supplies, planes, and ships to England to aid in its defense. Many Americans believed that passing this bill would be taking steps toward becoming involved in the "European" war. Margaret voted for this bill, with the belief that peace would not come by giving in.

Another hard choice before Margaret was the unpopular bill called the Selective Service and Training Act. This bill would call into military service nearly 900,000 young men between the ages of twenty-one and thirty-three. The idea of a peacetime draft law was entirely new. The United States was not involved in the war raging in Europe, and most Americans did not want to become involved! Many felt that the problems in Europe were none of their business, and were strongly opposed to drafting and training men to fight when the war was so far away. Only during major wars in the past had the country allowed mandatory service.

As a Republican and a woman, Margaret was expected to vote *against* putting young men into uniform and teaching them to use weapons. Because Margaret had been concerned about the nation's defense since 1938, she did the unexpected and voted for the bill!

Few remembered that in 1938, while her husband was still alive, Margaret had been asked to deliver a speech to the Kennebec County Women's Republican Club on October 27, which was Navy Day. As Congressman Smith's wife, she was invited to share some of the aspects of social life in Washington, D.C.

But Margaret, never one to give up an opportunity to make good use of her time, decided to highlight Navy Day by making a speech urging the strengthening of the Navy. She said, "Those who oppose Naval protection fail to perceive that the real attack, if any, will be by way of the sea."

She observed that the founding fathers of America had urged preparedness when it had taken months to cross the ocean. Now, when it could be done in a matter of hours, it was doubly important.

Margaret's audience may not have grasped the significance of her remarks that day, but they proved to be prophetic words!

It was interesting that about the same time Margaret gave her Navy Day speech, the Chairman of the House Naval Affairs Committee, Carl Vinson, was losing a strategic battle. He had asked the House of Representatives to raise money for the military fortification of a little Pacific island named Guam. He wanted Guam to be an American naval base. The members of the House of Representatives did not see the need, so they turned him down.

Finally in mid-September of 1940, the controversial Selective Service Act passed in the House of Representatives. Men began pouring into the induction centers. Many new units (artillery, tank, infantry) were being organized and training began.

Quite unexpectedly, Margaret's words spoken two years before came back to haunt her. On Sunday, December 7, 1941, Japanese war planes roared out of the sky in a surprise attack on the United States Pacific fleet anchored at Pearl Harbor on the Hawaiian Island of Oahu. Most of our ships were sunk, our planes were destroyed on the airfield, and over 2,000 Americans lost their lives. The war which had seemed so far away had landed right on our doorstep!

Four days later, on December 11, Hitler declared war on the United States. In return, President Roosevelt and Congress declared war on both Germany and Japan. The peace so many had carefully guarded was over.

Americans were of two opinions immediately following the sneak attack on Pearl Harbor. Some were irritated that the news had interrupted a radio broadcast of a football game! Others, when they finally heard the announcement, were infuriated that the so-called "inferior race" would dare attack the United States Navy.

Anger at the Japanese was intense, perhaps more so because this infamous deed could not be blamed on the Nazis. The focus of war had been on Hitler and the events in Europe until this point. President Roosevelt was committed to the European allies: England, France, and Russia. But Hitler's declaration of war gave the United States no choice. We were forced to begin fighting on *two* fronts: both in Europe and the Pacific. Americans became united in the effort to struggle and suffer for the national cause.

Margaret was particularly shaken by the destruction of the Pacific fleet. There was little comfort in knowing she had been right when she urged naval preparedness. The country was mistaken in assuming that we would never be attacked.

Three years after being elected to the House of Representatives, Margaret asked to be appointed to the House Naval Affairs Committee. This may have seemed like a strange request for a lady Senator to make, but she had a reason. Maine has a very long coastline and a major defense shipbuilding industry. Margaret's keen interest in the armed forces had continued (the Navy, in particular), and her request was granted. She began working on the major committee of her choice.

In 1945 Margaret was sent as the only woman with a group of other Congressmen to tour the South Pacific. They covered 25,000 miles by air in seventeen days and made fifteen stops. This was no vacation, there was a war still raging.

Margaret interviewed the nurses and wounded soldiers in the hospitals. On one island there were 45,000 men. They had done their best to fix a nice place for her to stay. Some of the soldiers had gone into the jungle and picked a handful of flowers for the table next to her cot. "These were the little things that touched my heart," Margaret recalls.

Those first few years as a legislator were teaching Margaret many things. She had to think through her beliefs on how to vote. There were times when she had to make difficult choices, but always voted what her conscience and research said was best.

"I tried to take the best from both Republican and Democratic ideas and put them together."

Margaret explains the voting process this way:

"There are a number of ways to determine how to vote. First and easiest is to vote which way the Party says. That is the lazy way, I could not do it. Second, vote the way your committee says. But that doesn't always work, since there are Congressmen from both large and small states, rich and not so rich, and with a variety of industry, or none. I could not always vote with my committee, since it would not have proven best for my district and my state. So, on the major issues, I got all the information I could find, educated myself, and voted the way I believed was right for my people and the nation as a whole."

"It would amuse me when people would ask me how I was going to vote the same day the issue came up. It might be months before the vote would be taken, how could I tell which way I was going to vote? Even if I knew, I wouldn't say. I never told ahead of time how I planned to vote."

As Margaret's years increased in the House of Representatives, so did her unbroken record of being present for every roll-call vote. There were times when votes were taken by a simple show of hands, but when the roll was called and each legislator present had to answer either "aye" or "nay," Margaret believed she should always be there to register her vote out loud.

When Margaret wasn't busy with legislative business, she would often travel back to Skowhegan for a quick visit with family and friends. Sometimes George and Carrie Chase or one of her sisters would come to Washington to visit Margaret. They would watch her at her seat on the House floor from the visitors gallery, or eat lunch with her in the dining room. But whenever people would brag about Margaret to her parents, Carrie would say, "I have three other children also, and I'm equally proud of them all."

Margaret did not boast about her own accomplishments either, but one crusade she carried on during her years in the House, did make her proud. Margaret sponsored a bill that provided improved status for women in the military.

Each branch of the military — Army, Navy, Air Force, and Marines — had an auxiliary for women. They did jobs such as air-traffic control, clerical work, and communications, so that the men would be free for active duty. These auxiliaries were considered reserves rather than regular military status. Therefore, the women who served were not entitled to full privileges and pay. Margaret could not accept this injustice. Her goal was to get permanent *regular* status for women in the services.

When it appeared that the bill would be stalled in committee discussion, she wrote a letter to the Secretary of Defense, James W. Forrestal, urging him to take a public stand. The letter got results. He immediately told the committee that the national military establishment felt it very important the women be granted permanent regular status in the Armed Service.[1]

In the early spring of 1948, Margaret began thinking of serving in the United States Senate. She had already served four terms (eight years), in the House of Representatives, and if she had been a man, she would have automatically been in line for the seat of Wallace W. White, the Senator who was now retiring.

---

[1] On a recent Sunday in 1988, women from Maine to California joined together at the Margaret Chase Smith Library Center in her hometown to honor her efforts in obtaining their place in the 1940's.

To Margaret, the issue was a simple one. She said the legislative action was long overdue. After the tribute by the lady veterans, Margaret responded by recalling her visit to the Pacific in 1945 and watching the Navy women, "working around the clock without thanks, without any of the benefits that go with regular service."

Her chances of being elected looked hopeless. The current governor of Maine, Horace Hildreth, had announced his intention to run. A former governor, Sumner Sewall, was also seeking a seat. In addition, a popular minister had decided to run. The field was crowded with male vote-getters. Many people advised her to be content where she was. Besides, they thought, even though there were one or two women in the Senate, three would definitely be too many!

Whenever anyone challenged Margaret by telling her she could not do something, she would set out to do it! She believed that because of her experience and legislative ability, she was best qualified for the job. She decided to offer herself as a candidate.

She was extremely busy in Washington and had very little time to campaign. But she committed herself to spend as many weekends as possible touring the state from Caribou to Kittery. She acted on a principle of Clyde's, that the only way to win an election was to meet as many people as possible. Her friends and supporters from former elections were helpful in arranging meetings at any available hall or school building. There, Margaret would explain her position on the issues and answer the voter's questions.

Margaret started her campaign with a pledge to the voters, "to be on the job in Washington and vote." She soon found out that one of her greatest assets was better than money or power, and that was friends! She had made many friends when she and Clyde had campaigned together, and these along with others had remained loyal throughout Margaret's four terms in the House.

She had been very active as a leader of the Maine Business and Professional Women's Club. This club, along with the Somerset County Women's Republican Club supported Margaret throughout her campaign.

She made no promises, but rather her campaign slogan was, "Don't Trade A Record For A Promise." Margaret started out driving herself to the various meetings, but after a mishap in Bangor, where she injured her arm, volunteers began driving for her.

Soon after the start of the campaign, an anonymous paper claiming to be a true record of Margaret's votes in the House of Representatives was circulated in Maine. The author of the paper was never discovered, but whoever it was tried to make it appear that Margaret voted for bills that would be helpful to the Communist cause. The paper also falsified her votes on major Republican issues. It was a deliberate attempt to spread lies about her.

This is called "smear tactics", but it did not work since any legislator's voting record can be easily checked.

Margaret was impatient to defend herself since she could easily have produced the facts of her voting record. But her campaign manager, William Lewis, urged her to wait until it was almost time for the June Primary to set the record straight. So she waited until May 21 to give a speech before the Somerset County Women's Republican Club. In it, she corrected each false charge item by item with the truth.

The evening before the Primary election was to take place, Margaret delivered a prepared statement over the radio, again placing her accurate voting record before the people of Maine. The results were that on Primary day the vote tally was:

Smith 63,786
Hildreth 30,949
Sewall 21,768
Beverage 6,399

Margaret was successful in the June Primary against three male candidates. Now, she faced her Democratic opponent in the September General Election. She campaigned as much as possible from June until Election Day. In all, she made appearances in six hundred towns during the campaign!

In 1948, Maine held its General Election in September. The news media was expecting an exciting climax to the campaign, and they arrived in Skowhegan in full force. The night of September 13 saw the Chase home, where Carrie Chase still lived since George Chase's death, mobbed with people. Newsmen, a television camera crew, friends, supporters, and campaign workers nearly filled the living room to capacity. The entire first floor had been turned into office space. Desks and tables were covered with mail. The doorbell rang constantly as well-wishers dropped by to say "good luck!"

Amid the noise and confusion, Margaret moved calmly about speaking to neighbors and friends, answering the telephone, dictating letters, and listening to the election returns as they were broadcast over the radio.

Her Democratic opponent was a Portland doctor. After her overwhelming victory in the June Primary, it was no surprise to most Mainers when Margaret won election to the Senate with over seventy-one percent of the vote!

Margaret had set another record. She was the first woman to be elected to BOTH the House of Representatives and the Senate.

Though fussed over by women's groups and played up to in the newspapers, Margaret knew she would have to be accepted in the Senate, not because she was a woman, but as a working lawmaker. Because of her work for the servicewomen in the past, it left the impression with some people that Margaret was a feminist, concentrating on legislation for women. She has been adamant in correcting this misconception.

"If there is any one thing I have attempted to avoid it is being a feminist. I definitely resent being called a feminist. I consider that women are people and that the record they make is a matter of ability and desire rather than of their sex. I came here as a United States Senator, not as a woman."

If people thought Margaret would just sit back after being elected to the Senate, they were wrong! She began her new career with the same outspoken honesty that had gained her a reputation for dealing directly with problems in the past. Margaret had always considered honesty more important than blind devotion to a political party. Her chin becomes firm as she states, "I was determined to keep my word to the people I served. I wouldn't give in once I'd made up my mind. I would always see a thing through."

Margaret deplores liars. "I wouldn't let them lie to me," she says. History attests to this. No matter how important anyone was in Washington, D.C., those who lied to Margaret Chase Smith never got away with it.

As a Senator, Margaret's work was greatly increased. There were times when hundreds of letters would pour into her office. Requests for her to speak at colleges, civic meetings, and business functions had to be arranged. Research into the many bills she would vote on needed to be done. These, along with other duties could have kept her from maintaining her unbroken roll call voting record.

Margaret was very proud of this record. When some other Senators felt free to campaign or take trips and leave the business they had been elected to do to others, Margaret remained in Washington to vote on the important issues.

In relation to her voting record, one New Hampshire newspaper editor said, "She's the Lou Gehrig of the Senate."

It was time for Margaret to find an assistant. She had been served during her Senate campaign by an able young lawyer whom she had met when she was a member of the House Naval Affairs Committee.

He was Major General William C. Lewis, known as "Bill" to his friends. He was well along on a military career that took him from Private in the Army, to Commander in the Navy, to Lieutenant General in the Air Force.

Bill was born in Wilburton, Oklahoma. He was known for his organizational talent, foresight, and humility. As a military professional, his ability as a strategist was highly respected. He enjoyed learning and studying about a wide range of subjects, including law, business administration, and geology. He had earned degrees in these areas.

Bill had received many military decorations including the Air Force Distinguished Service Medal, the Naval Legion of Merit, and the Army's Meritorious Service Medal.

When Bill Lewis was admitted to the United States Supreme Court Bar, following both his father and mother, it was the first time in the history of the Surpreme Court that an entire family had been admitted.

Bill Lewis more than filled the qualifications for the job as Margaret's assistant, and in 1949 he became her "right-hand man."

As Clyde Smith's wisdom and experience in politics had guided and influenced her early years, so Bill Lewis would have a major impact on her Senate years.

Margaret makes plans for the 1964 Presidential campaign with her executive assistant, Major General William C. Lewis, Jr.

VII

After the end of World War II, the United States and Russia became involved in what was called the "Cold War". Without guns, the Cold War was, nevertheless, a real battle. It was a battle of words, suspicions, smuggling military secrets, false accusations, and threats to our country's security.

During the war, Russia and the United States had been allies, but after victory over Hitler had been won, Russia began setting up Communist governments in East Germany, Czechoslovakia, Poland, and Hungary. Americans felt betrayed by the Russian government since American soldiers had given their lives to free the European countries from the Nazis. Now, it seemed those same countries were under domination by another oppressive power. Russian border guards kept watch over who came into or left the countries under Russian control.

Consequently, the relations between Russia and the United States became strained. After a few real cases of spying had been uncovered in Washington, many people seemed ready to believe there might be a spy behind every bush. The few who were caught giving or selling state secrets to our enemies aroused the indignation of the Junior Senator from Wisconsin, Joseph R. McCarthy.

Joe McCarthy was an obscure, unknown Senator until February 9, 1950, the day he delivered a public speech in Wheeling, West Virginia. With a look of dark anger, he held up an envelope which, he claimed, contained a list of persons who belonged to the Communist Party and who worked for the government of the United States.

The so-called "McCarthy Era" lasted about four years. During that time, many lives and reputations were shattered. At one point, Joe McCarthy claimed his list totaled more than 200 names! No one was exempt from his attacks. He was in a position to look into the past lives of a various group of Americans from movie actors, to newspaper columnists, to State Department employees. He mounted a campaign of accusing people at every level.

Margaret described the atmosphere in Washington this way: "Joe McCarthy had built up so much fear in people, they were not only afraid to talk, but they were afraid of whom they might be seen with."

Senator McCarthy supposedly had files thick with "proof" of his charges. But as time went on, it became clear to Margaret that this "proof" did not exist. Meanwhile, innocent people's lives and reputations were being ruined by lies. Margaret asked Senator McCarthy over and over again to produce concrete proof of his accusations, but he would merely smile mysteriously and tap the file folders on his desk.

One of the things that angered Margaret the most was

that Joe McCarthy was taking advantage of his immunity as a Senator to accuse innocent people and there was nothing they could do about it! Because he made his accusations in the Senate, his victims were powerless to stop him.

Margaret decided it was time someone spoke out against this terrible injustice. With the help of her assistant, Bill Lewis, she wrote the draft of a speech at her Skowhegan home on Memorial Day weekend. Six other Senators allowed her to include their names. Margaret and Bill Lewis returned to Washington on Memorial Day evening with the final draft.

After lunch on Thursday, June 1, 1950, Margaret and Bill Lewis left her office. Bill carried 200 mimeographed copies of the speech with instructions from Margaret not to pass them out until she started to speak.

As Bill and Margaret boarded the little subway train that carried Senators from their offices to the Capitol, Senator Joe McCarthy also got on board.

He said to Margaret, "You look very serious. Are you going to make a speech?"

Margaret said, "Yes, and you will not like it."

Joe smiled, "Is it about me?"

"Yes, but I am not going to mention your name," Margaret replied.

Joe frowned at that point and reminded Margaret that he controlled his home state's (Wisconsin) twenty-seven convention votes.

Margaret believed this was a thinly veiled threat that if she were to run for the office of Vice-President, she would not receive Wisconsin's support.

There was no more discussion as the subway train arrived at the Capitol.

Margaret sat quietly at her desk in the first row waiting for her turn to speak. Bill waited next to the wall near the desk holding the copies of her speech. When another Senator finished delivering his speech Margaret stood, waiting to be recognized. In her hand was her first major speech, which she called, "Declaration of Conscience."

Bill Lewis began handing out copies of the speech to the pages to be passed to the newsmen in the gallery.

Margaret was recognized by the Senate President, walked to the podium and began to read. True to her word, she mentioned no one by name, but everyone knew who she was speaking about when she said,

> "Those of us who shout the loudest about Americanism in making character assassinations are all too frequently those who, by our own words and acts, ignore some of the basic principles of Americanism:
>
> The right to criticize;
>
> The right to hold unpopular beliefs
>
> The right to protest;
>
> The right of independent thought,
>
> The exercise of these rights should not cost one single American citizen his reputation or his right to a livelihood..."

She continued,
> "Freedom of speech is not what it used to be in America. It has been so abused by some, that it is not exercised by others."

She ended with these words,
> "As an American, I want to see our nation recapture the strength and unity it once had when we fought the enemy instead of ourselves."

It seemed that everyone had a reaction to her speech! Senator McCarthy sat at his desk behind Margaret throughout her fifteen minute speech. When she finished, she sat down, expecting that he would make an answering speech. She waited, but he did not say a word. Instead, he quietly left the Senate.

The speech produced the heaviest mail Margaret ever received. It was eight to one in favor of the speech. Newspapers were overwhelmingly supportive, also. There were a few who condemned it with editorial comments or cartoons, some even suggested the speech had been written by someone else, and Margaret had just been asked to read it. For the most part, however, people realized the Senator from Maine had a mind of her own!

Many other interesting things happened as a result of the speech. Her picture was on the cover of *Newsweek* magazine and she was offered a commission as a Lieutenant Colonel in the Air Force Reserve. On Washington's birthday, the following February, she received a Freedom Foundation Award for the Declaration of Conscience. Most of all, people started taking the lady Senator from Maine seriously.

Some other things, not so pleasant, were also a result of her speech. Joe McCarthy tried to retaliate against her by getting her removed from two of the Senate Committees on which she served. He also supplied money and support for Margaret's opponent in the June, 1954 Maine State Primary Election. Margaret beat Joe's candidate by a margin of five to one, setting a new record of total votes cast in a primary election!

Soon after her election to the Senate, Margaret began writing a syndicated newspaper column which she called, "Washington and You." It was printed in thirty newspapers and circulated in sixteen states. In addition to all her other work, she continued to write the column for over five years.

For a long time Margaret had wanted to travel to other countries of the world to see how United States foreign aid money was being spent. She planned her trip for the fall and winter months of 1954. The Congress was in recess, so she would not miss any votes.

Her plan included visiting ten nations in Europe, including Spain, England, France, Germany, Russia and Switzerland. She paid all her own expenses and traveled like an average person, stopping at various places along the way to see and talk with ordinary people as well as the leaders of the different countries.

Her visit with Prime Minister and Lady Churchill of England centered on world peace. She listened to a speech by the Prime Minister, who had fiercely led his country to victory during the war. Winston Churchill hoped to complete his career by going down in history as the master architect of a permanent and lasting peace.

Margaret interrupted her trip in December to return to Washington for the Senate censure vote of Joseph R. McCarthy, in which the Senators in a 67 to 22 vote showed their disapproval of McCarthy's activities. It had taken over four years since Margaret's Declaration of Conscience speech for the Senate to finally express their objections of McCarthy. This proved that *many* people were afraid of him and his methods.

Margaret resumed her world tour in February, 1955. She visited leaders in many cities and villages in fourteen Asian and European countries. Margaret truly enjoyed her visit with school children and teachers in Turkey, Thailand, India, and Taiwan.

She began a friendship with the wife of the President of Taiwan, Madam Chiang-Kai-shek, that has continued through the years.

It was in 1958 that Russia shocked the world with the launch of the first unmanned space flight, called *Sputnik*. The Congress immediately created a Senate Aeronautical and Space Sciences Committee. Because of her seniority, Margaret was given a choice of remaining on the Government Operations Committee or filling a seat on the new Space Committee. She chose the Space Committee, which proved to be one the most interesting and successful assignments during her years in the Senate.

Space was a new venture for the United States. Only a handful of military scientists had been conducting experiments, but now billions of dollars would be appropriated to create the National Aeronautics and Space Administration (NASA). Margaret's role on the committee would be as a "watchdog" to make sure the money was spent wisely and that the very best people would be in charge of the program. In the process of interviewing and listening to testimony about the space program, she became acquainted with many of the astronauts from Project Mercury up through the Apollo flights. When Apollo 10 lifted off the launch pad on May 18, 1969, a special pin with her name on it was aboard the space craft.

In May, 1969 this pin was carried into lunar orbit aboard Apollo 10 for Margaret.

VIII

"Why don't you run for President, Margaret?" This question came to Senator Smith from many people during the early part of 1963. At first, she did not take it seriously, since for several years her name had been mentioned as a possible Vice-Presidential candidate. But now her mail was increasing with that intriguing question occurring more often.

Margaret had finally been persuaded to announce the decision at the Woman's National Press Club meeting in Washington on December 5, 1963. But on the afternoon of November 22, the activities of the nation stood still as the news spread that President John F. Kennedy had been shot and killed in Dallas, Texas.

Kennedy was a popular Democratic President. He had served three years of his first four-year term. The country was plunged into shock over his death. Strangers wept together on the streets when they heard the news.

For three days after the assassination, the public was submitted to more shocks. As viewers watched on television, the alleged assassin named Lee Harvey Oswald, was also shot and killed by a night-club owner, Jack Ruby, right under the noses of the Dallas police.

A horrified and grief-stricken country watched as President Kennedy's funeral was broadcast over live television. For the first time in recent history, the death of a president was brought into the living rooms of America. Thousands of viewers watched the events almost non-stop for three days. It was horrible, yet fascinating to feel a part of what was happening.

Vice-President Lyndon B. Johnson was sworn in as President only minutes after the death of Kennedy. He smoothly took charge of the government, but there was a sense of nightmare unreality to the following days.

Margaret immediately cancelled all of her public appearances out of respect to the slain President.

She rescheduled her Press Club appointment for January 27, 1964. Meanwhile, the news media tried many approaches to get her or her aides to "spill the beans" with an early announcement. But she kept her silence.

Margaret wrote the speech with two endings. One, "I will not run." The other, "I will run." Even Bill Lewis didn't know her decision so he could honestly tell the newsmen that he didn't know!

Margaret began her speech at one o'clock in the afternoon. She devoted the major portion of her speech to the reasons why she should and should not run for President. She listed the following reasons why she SHOULD run:

She had more public office experience than any of the other candidates. She would be pioneering the way for a woman to be elected President. Her candidacy would give the voters more of a choice. Her independence gave her freedom from any political pressure groups, consequently, she would be indebted to no one.

She went on to the reasons why she SHOULD NOT run:

Some people had advised her that no woman should dare to run for President. Her chances of winning were hopeless. As a woman, it was feared she would not have the physical stamina for the campaign. She had no money. In the past, she had paid election expenses out of her own pocket. She had no big political organization, only unpaid volunteers. If she left the Senate for long periods of time to campaign, her roll-call vote record would be broken.

She concluded, "So because of these reasons against my running, I have decided that I SHALL enter the New Hampshire Presidential Primary. . ." Margaret had waited right up until she was actually reading the line in her speech before she chose which ending to use! The audience roared with delight. They were happy with her decision, as well as the way she had kept them in suspense.

Margaret had no illusions about the challenge she had just committed herself to. She knew that without the financial backing or the political support of the majority of people, she literally had no chance of being elected President. But, she felt that her attempt would bring an opportunity to women in the field of public service that had been denied them for a long time.

Margaret also believed her candidacy for President

would be a test to see how much support she would receive by running on the same principles she had always stood for since her first campaign in 1940 for the House of Representatives.

Reflecting back on her decision to run she says, "Some people wanted me to run for President. I finally gave in, but I didn't have any money . . . I never accepted money. I knew I couldn't get very far without it."

She campaigned in New Hampshire on two separate weekends, shaking hands, speaking to groups, visiting factories, schools, and businesses. The people were warm and friendly, even though one day the temperature was twenty-eight degrees below zero!

Margaret's first stop was Pittsburg in the northernmost section of New Hampshire. Two loggers loading pulp wood in the snow were startled to see Margaret out so early on a freezing cold morning.

"You've got a lot of zip to be up at this time in the morning," logger Almon Young told her.

When the votes were counted on primary day, March 10, she had come in fifth. But three other candidates polled fewer votes than Margaret. It was disappointing, but at the same time proved her point that voters wanted a wider choice of candidates. The man who had polled the most votes wasn't even on the ballot! He was a write-in candidate, Henry Cabot Lodge Jr., who was serving an appointment as Ambassador to Vietnam.

April 14 was set as primary day in Illinois. Here Senator Smith had a group of dedicated women volunteers who poured their time and energy into her campaign. Again, Margaret was able to spend a limited time in the state, but she used every minute in speeches, television talk shows, and meeting the voters.

When all the votes were counted, Margaret had won thirty percent of the vote, instead of the ten percent that had been predicted. This surprise result was possible with a meager expense of less than one thousand dollars!

The Oregon Primary was next. The state was three thousand miles from Washington, which was so far, any travel would disrupt her duty of voting in the Senate. In addition, lack of money hindered her candidacy. But, the volunteers were creative! They originated the "Margaret Chase Smith for President" button which became the prize button of 1964. Before the campaign ended the bidding price for a Rose-Signature campaign button reached $25.00! Even though Margaret didn't go to Oregon in person, her message was spread by the lady volunteers.

As in New Hampshire, she came in fifth in Oregon. But she also picked up several thousand write-in votes in the Texas, Massachusetts, and Pennsylvania primaries.

The Republican National Convention, where the winner would be nominated for President, was held in San Francisco, California. On Sunday, June 12, 1964, a smiling Margaret arrived at the San Francisco airport. A large, enthusiastic crowd greeted her with signs and banners proclaiming, MARGARET FOR PRESIDENT. In the background, a band played "Hello Maggie."

On the day the nomination for President was to take

place, thousands of delegates from all over the United States were packed into the auditorium. Newsmen, commentators, and technicians were crowding every inch of space.

Margaret broke the unwritten rule that Presidential candidates be absent when their nomination speech is made. (Every other candidate before and since has either stayed at home to await the outcome, or in recent years, watched the event on television from their hotel room.) But Margaret wanted to be where the action was! In a simple, bright red dress, the traditional rose on her left shoulder, she sat in the Smith box surrounded by friends and supporters.

Her nomination speech was delivered by an old friend and admirer, Senator George D. Aiken of Vermont. Senator Aiken's speech was clear and direct, a masterpiece of New England simplicity.

This is part of what he said:

"Mr. Chairman and Delegates:

I intend to nominate for President one of the most capable persons I have ever known and one with whom I have been associated in public service for twenty-four years.

I don't like to start a nominating speech with a confession, but the circumstances are compelling.

In introducing my candidate, I find myself in a most peculiar position, I am severely restricted in what I can offer for your support.

I can't promise you a cabinet job, an ambassador's appointment, or even a shot at a nice government contract.

I can't even offer you cigars or chewing gum. For awhile it looked real promising. I thought I could at least invite you all out for coffee because I knew my candidate was having checks and $10.00 and $1.00 bills and pennies sent her from most every State in the Union.

Pennies came in from school children, and dollars from low income people who couldn't afford it. Then there were some beautiful checks in three and four figures from real important business people.

The outlook was as rosy as a Pacific sunset as portrayed by the Chamber of Commerce. You and I were going to have a wonderful time here in San Francisco.

Then do you know what happened? Do you know what my candidate pulled on me?

She took every big check, every little check, every $10.00 bill, every $1.00 bill, every penny, and sent them straight back to where they came from.

My candidate wants the nomination solely on her record and her qualifications for the job. As a result, our transportation fund is busted. Our entertainment fund is shattered. Our demonstration wallet collapsed. Our conscience is intact.

That's why I can't offer you any candy or cigars or chewing gum or even ask you all out for a cup of coffee.

The only thing left in the world for me to offer you for your support is the best managed government the United States ever had — a government headed by the best qualified person you ever voted for."

Senator Aiken then went on to list five qualifications for the office of President that he believed a candidate should have:

"1. *A President should have integrity.*

Whether dealing with foreign nations or the folks back home, integrity is a priceless asset. My candidate stands ace high in this respect.

2. *A President should have ability.*

Good intentions alone are not enough. We don't want the floors of the White House paved with good intentions. If my candidate does not have the ability, then the forty-four universities and colleges that have awarded her degrees based solely on merit have been wrong.

3. *A President should have had wide experience in government.*

If twenty-four years experience on the roughest, toughest committees of the Congress, Defense, Space, Appropriations, Government Operations and Rules don't qualify my candidate, then the other candidates whose names are being submitted to you cannot possibly be qualified, for none of them can approach her record.

4. *A President should have courage* — courage to

stand for the right when it may not be popular to do so — courage to stand for decency in the conduct of public affairs — courage to stand alone if necessary against formidable odds. Does my candidate have this kind of courage? I can refer you to several high ranking officers of the United States Armed Forces who have learned from experience that she is ably qualified in this respect. As a sincere testimonial to her courage the Reserve Officers Association has recently designated her as "Minute Man of the Year" — the first time this great honor has ever been conferred upon a person of her sex.

5. *A President should have common sense.*

My candidate stands par excellence in this respect. Time and again I have seen her keep her head "when all about her were losing theirs" and blaming it on everyone but themselves. She wants to get things done that ought to be done and she wants them done right. She does not panic when things don't go to suit her. She just keeps on headed for her goal — which at this moment is the Republican nomination for the Presidency."

Senator Aiken continued on to state many other qualities that Margaret possessed. As he reached the conclusion of the nominating speech he said, "I am now proud to nominate that candidate — the Senior Senator from the Great Republican State of Maine — Senator Smith."

At the end of his speech, the cheerleaders and demonstrators marched out onto the floor. Margaret's demonstration was organized by the volunteers. School children dressed in matching outfits and straw hats, waving banners, paraded around the arena singing, while the band played. Margaret beamed from her seat as the huge delegation expressed their respect and affection for the gallant lady from Maine.

"My campaign showed what a group of dedicated women volunteers could do. They worked very, very, hard," Margaret recalled.

Margaret did not win the Presidential nomination that night. It was a foregone conclusion that Senator Barry Goldwater would be the Republican Party's choice for President. Nevertheless, it was a moment in history never repeated.

The Rose-Signature campaign button.

IX

The 1960's brought troubled times to the United States. Many areas of the South were experiencing upheaval. Blacks were struggling for the right to vote. They wanted the same fair and equal treatment that whites received when riding buses, eating at lunch counters, and using public restrooms. They believed they had been denied these constitutional rights for too long.

Whites and blacks had been segregated into separate schools and neighborhoods. Blacks were forced to ride at the rear of buses, usually standing up, and were expected to submit silently when being abused. Large groups of blacks and sympathetic whites marched into southern cities to attract attention to their cause.

Some dark chapters were written in American history during the hot summers of the 1960's. What began as peaceful demonstrations, sit-ins, and marches turned to violence as time passed with little visible change.

In addition, the United States had slowly become involved in a war in a small Asian country called Vietnam. Young people, particularly college students, began to protest the United States participation in the war.

Margaret meeting Chancellor Conrad Adenauer of West Germany and his daughter.

Margaret interviewed Generalissimo Franco, President of Spain, through an interpreter on her world tour.

Margaret in discussion with Dwight D. Eisenhower.

Left to right in front row: Senator Edmund Muskie, Margaret and Represenative Clifford McIntyre, all of Maine, listen to President John F. Kennedy deliver a speech, July, 1963.

Margaret being escorted by President Lyndon B. Johnson to a luncheon, October 14, 1966.

Margaret listens attentively to President Richard M. Nixon at the White House, June 3, 1971.

Left to right: Captain Gus Grissom, Colonel John Glenn and Margaret after Friendship Seven space shot in 1962.

In 1962 Margaret visited the naval base at Guantanamo Bay, Cuba.

On January 27, 1964 Margaret announced her intention to run for President of the United States.

The demonstration for Margaret at the 1964 Republican Convention, San Francisco, California.

Margaret and Senator John Stennis of Mississippi.

Margaret preparing for her flight aboard an F-100 Super Sabre jet.

Margaret and Senator Barry Goldwater (R.) from Arizona at the 1963 Senate Republican Conference.

Senator Everett Dirkson (R.) from Illinois confers with Margaret.

Margaret checks the view through a periscope during her three hour trip aboard the submarine, U.S.S. Permit, 1969.

Margaret at work on the Appropriations Sub Committee in May, 1964.

The "equal rights" demonstrations, combined with those protesting the Vietnam war, caused the worst upheaval in American life since the Civil War.

Not only was the country changing, but Maine, Margaret's home state was changing also. Maine had boasted a large number of industries . . . logging and paper, shoes and textiles, agriculture and ship building. In spite of Senator Smith's attempts in the Senate to get bills passed that would safeguard the smaller industrial states, unrestricted trade between nations was encouraged. Many cheaper foreign products were being shipped into this country. Americans were buying these less expensive goods instead of those made in the United States. Consequently, many Maine industries were going out of business and workers no longer had jobs.

These were some of the issues heard in the spring of 1972 as Robert Monks challenged Senator Smith for the Republican nomination for the Senate from Maine. She had considered retirement so she could devote full time to speaking, writing, and organizing her papers.

Over the years she had saved every letter, memo, newspaper clipping, and speech. Margaret wanted to organize all of this material and find a way for it to be used properly.

She had already invested a great deal of time and energy writing a book, *Declaration of Conscience,* published in 1972. The book, titled the same as her 1950 speech, described her struggles as she fought for what she believed. It also included some of her major speeches on the important issues of the times. Margaret's assistant, Bill Lewis, edited the book and added his personal commentary at the end of each chapter.

But when Robert Monks claimed that at age seventy-four she was no longer able to continue the strenuous work of a Senator, she decided to run for a fifth term. She did not want the voters to think his challenge was scaring her into retirement.

Monks was thirty-eight years old, handsome, and a millionaire. The issues he brought up before the June Primary included: the need for a decent living for senior citizens, the problem of defense contracts going to other states rather than Maine, over-fishing in the North Atlantic (which many people felt would deplete the ocean's resources), the drug and environmental issues, and Senator Smith's age.

Robert Monks said that she had neglected the vital interests of Maine people to concentrate on national issues. Monks was a businessman and had never served in an elected public office. He claimed he would defeat Margaret with time and money.

Margaret stood behind her voting record in the Senate, instead of defending herself against his remarks. She felt that what she had accomplished would speak for itself.

Although Robert Monks waged an expensive campaign, Margaret defeated him by two to one margin in the June Primary.

The next test was in the November general election against the Democratic opponent, William Hathaway.

William Hathaway was a Massachusetts native who had settled in Auburn, Maine. He too was a wealthy businessman. He had already served eight years in the United States House of Representatives. Hathaway also made Margaret's age a major issue of the campaign.

He believed the work she was doing on the various committees, such as the Space Committee, did not benefit the people of Maine. He claimed that Mainers needed someone young with fresh ideas to represent them in the Senate. He cited the examples of "declining industry and people without jobs," things that "Senator Smith had done very little to correct."

On Sunday, November 5, Senator Smith and William Hathaway met on the Maine Public Broadcasting Network for a televised debate.

Margaret felt that she did well on the debate. She was calm and well-informed on the issues that were discussed.

Another of William Hathaway's charges against Margaret was that she depended too much on her assistant, Bill Lewis. Hathaway, commenting on his staff said, "I rely on my staff for research and in other background areas. I do not allow them to think for me."

Margaret's remarks on the subject were, "Bill Lewis and the rest of my staff do the research, the leg-work for me. That's what they are being paid to do. Bill often said to me, 'Senator, I have given you all the information I can find, but when you are out on the Senate floor, ready to vote, you are on your own.'

"Staffs are to use . . . he is a very able man, very helpful," Margaret stated.

After having worked with a staff for over thirty years, Margaret had this to say, "A public official is only as good as the people they have to assist them. Education, common sense and loyalty are very important."

Even though William Hathaway spent nearly a quarter of a million dollars to Margaret's twelve thousand, she continued her usual strategy, campaigning on weekends and during the Congressional recess. "I could not allow his challenge to force me to change the way I had conducted myself all those years. The people had confidence in me."

Some believe that many Maine voters did not bother to go to the polls, thinking that Margaret would win easily as she had in the past. On election day, Senator Smith was defeated (by less than 40,000 votes) for the first time in over thirty-two years in public office.

"I felt if that's what the people wanted, I was ready to abide by it. I'd served a long time . . . and I had served to the best of my ability. I was ready to do something else," she stated.

Margaret had been in Washington while six Presidents had been in office: Franklin Roosevelt, Harry Truman, Dwight Eisenhower, John Kennedy, Lyndon Johnson, and Richard Nixon.

She had traveled around the world. She had met and talked to great leaders and common people in many countries. She had made friends for the United States from England to India. In addition, Margaret had broken the sound barrier aboard a U.S. Air Force F-100 Super Sabre fighter. She spent three and one-half hours under the Pacific Ocean in a U.S. Navy submarine. She had exerted a major influence on the Space Program.

Margaret also had many firsts! The first woman to be elected to both the House of Representatives and the Senate. The first woman civilian to sail aboard a Navy destroyer during wartime. The first woman to address the Parliament of Iran. The first woman to run for President of the United States from a major political party.

Margaret had seen wars, poverty, protests . . . and peace. Few other women of the Twentieth Century have achieved the stature and respect of their nation as has Margaret Chase Smith.

Margaret shares a little advice as she has reached her nineties with fairly good health and abundant energy. "I have great energy because I love life. I ignore my age," she says.

X

Back home again! Margaret and her staff had packed everything in her Senate office to be shipped to Skowhegan. What would she do with all the books, papers, memos, and gifts? What would happen to these pieces of history? A thirty-two year collection needed plenty of space!

Bill Lewis had a dream of turning her vast collection into a permanent library. It was due to his foresight and under his guidance that the Margaret Chase Smith Library Center Foundation was established. Bill was so committed to the dream that he gave his own property to the Foundation in order that the money from it could be used to help fund the library.

It was far from easy for the members of the Foundation to choose between the various colleges that vied for the privilege of storing and using Senator Smith's papers. But in 1979, Margaret's house on Neil Hill, overlooking the Kennebec River, was deeded to the Northwood Institute. Northwood is an accredited college specializing in business management, with campuses in Michigan, Texas, and Florida. Northwood had agreed to receive Margaret's papers, raise money and build a library on the Skowhegan property.

Building plans were moving along with a completion date targeted for the summer of 1982. The design for the Library Center was to connect the new building to Margaret's own home by a series of hallways which would be a part of the display areas for the museum. Margaret and Bill liked the plan.

In May, they went to inspect the building progress. Two days later, Bill died of a heart attack. He did not live to see the fulfillment of their dream.

Bill's death was a great shock and loss to Margaret as they had enjoyed a very productive working relationship for over forty years.

Bill was admired and respected by a multitude of friends and associates. His funeral took place at the nation's National Cemetery in Arlington, Virginia on June 1, 1982.

On August 26, 1982, Margaret was joined by over one thousand friends, relatives, and associates for the dedication ceremony of the Library Center.

Margaret fought back the tears as she spoke on what she called, "A very meaningful day for me."

Today, the Margaret Chase Smith Library Center is one of the few outstanding Senatorial research library/museums in the country, but it is even more than that.

A typical day at the Library will bring groups of visitors and families to tour the museum. At the wide windows overlooking the parking area and flower beds, one or two researchers may be using the computer consoles to retrieve stored information. In the adjoining conference room, with its spectacular view of the river, a college researcher may be poring over files and scrapbooks piled high on the gleaming table. Busy staff members bring stacks of newspaper clippings and bulging file folders to a biographer studying in another corner.

The airy, spacious halls and display areas are built around a flowering patio. Sunlight streams through tall windows and effective lighting shows each display in the shining glass cases to full advantage. The displays are on child level, but are easily viewed by adults. The photos, artifacts, and mementos are constantly being added to and circulated. Displayed in one area are the ninety-two colorful satin hoods that have been awarded to Margaret with honorary degrees from colleges and universities throughout the country.

The contents of one case, containing a collection of roses made of various materials, is extra special to Margaret since it is the result of a "good natured battle" that lasted for thirty years!

Starting in the 1950's, Margaret introduced a bill in the Senate each year trying to get the rose named as the official flower of the United States. But another powerful Senator liked the marigold, so year after year the contest went on.

After she left the Senate, others took up the cause for the rose. It wasn't until 1986 that the House of Representatives passed the first bill officially naming the rose. Later the bill was passed in the Senate, and in October, 1987 President Ronald Reagan signed the bill which formally declared the rose the official flower of the United States.

Margaret was very pleased that her beloved rose had finally received its well-deserved honor. Smiling, she said, "I personally have nothing against marigolds, but I think roses smell better!"

In late June, 1989, Margaret received another surprise. She was invited to the White House to be the recipient of the Presidential Medal of Freedom. This is the highest civilian honor given in the United States, and is awarded to persons who have made outstanding contributions to: 1) the security or national interests of the United States; 2) world peace; or 3) cultural or other significant public or private endeavors.

This was formerly known as the Medal of Freedom but was renamed the Presidential Medal of Freedom by President John Kennedy on February 22, 1963. He chose a group of recipients, but did not live to make the awards.

It was on the morning of July 6, 1989 that Margaret stood with the other recipients at a White House ceremony in Washington, D.C. to receive her award from President George Bush. Margaret was deeply moved as President Bush spoke these words, "You have left an indelible mark as you have enriched this nation, and America is grateful."

Epilogue

. . . Margaret's hour with the school children has passed quickly with an animated question and answer session around the table. She is pleased with their responses, showing that they were prepared with background information before their arrival. As Margaret expected, the museum tour aroused great curiosity and many enthusiastic comments.

It's nearly time to go. The children gather in front of the bookshelves for a photo with the Senator. Handshakes and "good-byes" are repeated as the children reluctantly leave.

She turns back toward her office to start the morning routine of reading mail and answering telephone calls. But the halls seem to echo with the whispered conversation and laughter of children. Margaret smiles, already thinking about the next group that will be coming.

THE END

The Margaret Chase Smith Library Center, Skowhegan, Maine.

A view of the Margaret Chase Smith Library Center main exhibit gallery showing a portion of her 92 Doctoral hoods.

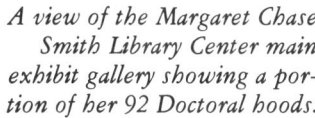

Left to right: Kristy Gervais, Amy Nadeau, and Robert Nadeau listen to Margaret explain the significance of the Presidential Medal of Freedom, August 4, 1989.

Margaret saying "good bye" to visitors.

THE FULL TEXT OF SENATOR SMITH'S MOST FAMOUS SPEECH

"Mr. President, I would like to speak briefly and simply about a serious national condition. It is a national feeling of fear and frustration that could result in national suicide and the end of everything that we Americans hold dear. It is a condition that comes from the lack of effective leadership in either the Legislative Branch or the Executive Branch of our Government.

That leadership is so lacking that serious and responsible proposals are being made that national advisory commissions be appointed to provide such critically needed leadership.

I speak as briefly as possible because too much harm has already been done with irresponsible words of bitterness and selfish political opportunism. I speak as simply as possible because the issue is too great to be obscured by eloquence. I speak simply and briefly in the hope that my words will be taken to heart.

I speak as a Republican. I speak as a woman. I speak as a United States Senator. I speak as an American.

The United States Senate has long enjoyed worldwide respect as the greatest deliberative body in the world. But recently that deliberative character has too often been debased to the level of a forum of hate and character assassination sheltered by the shield of Congressional immunity.

It is ironical that we Senators can in debate in the Senate directly or indirectly, by any form of words, impute to any American who is not a Senator any conduct or motive unworthy or unbecoming an American — and without that non-Senator American having any legal redress against us — yet if we say the same thing in the Senate about our colleagues we can be stopped on the grounds of being out of order.

It is strange that we can verbally attack anyone else without restrain and with full protection and yet we hold ourselves above the same type of criticism here on the Senate Floor. Surely the United States Senate is big enough to take self-criticism and self-appraisal. Surely we should be able to take the same kind of character attacks that we "dish out" to outsiders.

I think that it is high time for the United States Senate and its members to do some soul-searching — for us to weight our consciences — on the manner in which we are performing our duty to the people of America — on the manner in which we are using or abusing our individual powers and privileges.

I think that it is high time that we remembered that we have sworn to uphold and defend the Constitution. I think that it is high time that we remembered that the Constitution, as amended, speaks not only of the freedom of speech but also of trial by jury instead of trial by accusation.

Whether it be a criminal prosecution in court or a character prosecution in the Senate, there is little practical distinction when the life of a person has been ruined.

Those of us who shout the loudest about Americanism in making character assassinations are all too frequently those who, by our own words and acts, ignore some of the basic principles of Americanism:

The right to criticize;

The right to hold unpopular beliefs;

The right to protest;

The right of independent thought.

The exercise of these rights should not cost one single American citizen his reputation or his right to a livelihood nor should he be in danger of losing his reputation or livelihood merely because he happens to know someone who holds unpopular beliefs. Who of us doesn't? Otherwise none of us could call our souls our own. Otherwise thought control would have set in.

The American people are sick and tired of being afraid to speak their minds lest they be politically smeared as "Communists" or "Fascists" by their opponents. Freedom of speech is not what it used to be in America. It has been so abused by some that it is not exercised by others.

The American people are sick and tired of seeing innocent people smeared and guilty people whitewashed. But there have been enough proved cases, such as the Amerasia case, the Hiss case, the Coplon case, the Gold case, to cause nationwide distrust and strong suspicion that there may be something to the unproved, sensational accusations.

As a Republican, I say to my colleagues on this side of the aisle that the Republican Party faces a challenge today that is not unlike the challenge that it faced back in Lincoln's day. The Republican Party so successfully met that challenge that it emerged from the Civil War as the champion of a united nation — in addition to being a Party that unrelentingly fought loose spending and loose programs.

Today our country is being psychologically divided by the confusion and the suspicions that are bred in the United States Senate to spread like cancerous tentacles of "knowing nothing, suspect everything" attitudes. Today we have a Democratic Administration that has developed a mania for loose spending and loose programs. History is repeating itself — and the Republican Party again has the opportunity to emerge as the champion of unity and prudence.

The record of the present Democratic Administration has provided us with sufficient campaign issues without the necessity of resorting to political smears. America is rapidly losing its position as leader of the world simply because the Democratic Administration has pitifully failed to provide effective leadership.

The Democratic Administration has completely confused the American people by its daily contradictory grave warnings and optimistic assurances — that show the people that our Democratic Administration has no idea of where it is going.

The Democratic Administration has greatly lost the confidence of the American people by its complacency to the threat of Communism here at home and the leak of vital secrets to Russia through key officials of the Democratic Administration. There are enough proved cases to make this point without diluting our criticism with unproved charges.

Surely these are sufficient reasons to make it clear to the American people that it is time for a change and that a Republican victory is necessary to the security of this country. Surely it is clear that this nation will continue to suffer as long as it is governed by the present ineffective Democratic Administration.

Yet to displace it with a Republican regime embracing a philosophy that lacks political integrity or intellectual honesty would prove equally disastrous to this nation. The nation sorely needs a Republican victory. But I don't want to see the Republican Party ride to political victory on the Four Horsemen of Calumny — Fear, Ignorance, Bigotry, and Smear.

I doubt if the Republican Party could — simply because I don't believe the American people will uphold any political party that puts political exploitation above national interest. Surely we Republicans aren't that desperate for victory.

I don't want to see the Republican Party win that way. While it might be a fleeting victory for the Republican Party, it would be a more lasting defeat for the American people. Surely it would be a more lasting defeat for the American people. Surely it would ultimately be suicide for the Republican Party and the two-party system that has protected our American liberties from the dictatorship of a one party system.

As members of the Minority Party, we do not have the primary authority to formulate the policy of our Government. But we do have the responsibility of rendering constructive criticism, of clarifying issues, of allaying fears by acting as responsible citizens.

As a woman, I wonder how the mothers, wives, sisters and daughters feel about the way in which members of their families have been politically mangled in Senate debate — and I use the word "debate" advisedly.

As a United States Senator, I am not proud of the way in which the Senate has been made a publicity platform for irresponsible sensationalism. I am not proud of the reckless abandon in which unproved charges have been hurled from this side of the aisle. I am not proud of the obviously staged, undignified counterchanges that have been attempted in retaliation from the other side of the aisle.

I don't like the way the Senate has been made a rendezvous for vilification, for selfish and political gain at the sacrifice of individual reputations and national unity. I am not proud of the way we smear outsiders from the Floor of the Senate and hide behind the cloak of Congressional immunity and still place ourselves beyond criticism on the Floor of the Senate.

As an American, I am shocked at the way Republicans and Democrats alike are playing directly into the Communist design of "confuse, divide, and conquer." As an American, I don't want a Democratic Administration "whitewash" or "cover-up" any more than I want a Republican smear or witch hunt.

As an American, I condemn a Republican "Fascist" just as much as I condemn a Democrat "Communist". I condemn a Democrat "Fascist" just as much as I condemn a Republican "Communist." They are equally dangerous to you and me and to our country. As an American, I want to see our nation recapture the strength and unity it once had when we fought the enemy instead of ourselves.

It is with these thoughts that I have drafted what I call a "Declaration of Conscience." I am gratified that Senator Tobey, Senator Aiken, Senator Morse, Senator Ives, Senator Thye, and Senator Hendrickson have concurred in that declaration and have authorized me to announce their concurrence.

STATEMENT OF SEVEN REPUBLICAN SENATORS

1. We are Republicans. But we are Americans first. It is as Americans that we express our concern with the growing confusion that threatens the security and stability of our country. Democrats and Republicans alike have contributed to that confusion.

2. The Democratic Administration has initially created the confusion by its lack of effective leadership, by its con-

tradictory grave warnings and optimistic assurances, by its complacency to the threat of Communisim here at home, by its oversensitiveness to rightful criticism, by its petty bitterness against its critics.

3. Certain elements of the Republican Party have materially added to this confusion in the hopes of riding the Republican Party to victory through the selfish political exploitation of fear, bigotry, ignorance, and intolerance. There are enough mistakes of the Democrats for Repubicans to criticize constructively without resorting to political smears.

4. To this extent, Democrats and Republicans alike have unwittingly, but undeniably, played directly into the Communist design of "confuse, divide, and conquer".

5. It is high time that we stopped thinking politically as Republicans and Democrats about elections and started thinking patriotically as Americans about national security based on individual freedom. It is high time that we all stopped being tools and victims of totalitarian techniques — techniques that, if continued here unchecked, will surely end what we have come to cherish as the American way of life."

> Margaret Chase Smith, *Maine*
> Charles W. Tobey, *New Hampshire*
> George D. Aiken, *Vermont*
> Wayne L. Morse, *Oregon*
> Irving M. Ives, *New York*
> Edward J. Thye, *Minnesota*
> Robert C. Hendrickson, *New Jersey*

BIBLIOGRAPHY

Fleming, Alice, *The Senator From Maine*, Thomas Y. Crowell Co., New York, 1969.

Smith, Margaret Chase, *Declaration of Conscience*, Doubleday & Co. Inc., New York, 1972.

White, Theodore H., *The Making of the President 1964*, Atheneum Pub., New York, 1966.

Manchester, William, *The Glory and the Dream, A Narrative History of America 1932-1972,* Little Brown and Co., Boston, 1973.

Morin, Relman, *Dwight D. Eisenhower, A Gauge of Greatness*, Associated Press, 1969.

Borthick, David and Britton, Jack, *Medals, Military and Civilian of the United States*, M.C.N. Press, Tulsa, Oklahoma, 1984.

Acknowledgements

Without a support group of professionals and friends, an amateur writer could not reach the goal of a completed work. Therefore, it is with deep appreciation that I thank the following:

Senator Margaret Chase Smith for her openness in sharing herself with us.

The amiable and efficient Director of the Margaret Chase Smith Library Center, Greg Gallant, and his supportive staff for hours spent reading the manuscript, interviews, research, photo selection, and all the "extras".

Ginny Smith for her conscientious and able editing of the manuscript for appropriate language and development.

Senator George Mitchell of Maine for his willingness to write the foreword tribute.

Prudy McMann, Carol Cooley, and Jody Peterson for invaluable advice, research, typing, and encouragement.

The research staff at the Maine State Library.

Last, but not least, my eternal thanks to my long-suffering husband, Ray.

PHOTO CREDITS: The Margaret Chase Smith Library Center; The U.S. Senate-Historical Office (photo of Joseph McCarthy); Ron Maxwell of the *Central Maine Morning Sentinel*; Patricia Nadeau, my "personal photographer" and friend; *The Bangor Daily News*.

About the Author

Alberta Gould is a wife and the mother of two grown daughters. She is a reading tutor in the school district in her home town, Skowhegan, Maine.

Her interest in history coupled with that of children's literature has been the incentive for writing this, her first book.